EASY EATS

Cheap EATS

by Katrina Jorgensen

CAPSTONE PRESS
a capstone imprint

Dabble Lab is published by Capstone Press, an imprint of Capstone.
1710 Roe Crest Drive
North Mankato, Minnesota 56003
www.capstonepub.com

Library of Congress Cataloging-in-Publication Data is available on the Library of Congress website.
ISBN: 978-1-4966-8100-3 (hardcover)
ISBN: 978-1-4966-8104-1 (eBook PDF)

Summary: Delicious food doesn't have to be expensive! Make tasty meals with ingredients that are commonly found in the pantry. Simple, budget-friendly meals will teach kids how to create the classics without breaking the bank.

Image Credits
All photos by Capstone Studio: Karon Dubke

Design Elements: Shutterstock

Editorial Credits
Editor: Mari Bolte; Designer: Sarah Bennett; Media Researcher: Eric Gohl;
Production Specialist: Katy LaVigne; Photo Stylist: Sarah Schuette

Printed in the United States 4638

Contents

Introduction

Staring into a pantry full of food but still don't know what to make? Tired of eating the same things over and over? No time to run to the store? Gather the ingredients for a yummy new recipe with things you already have on hand! Make easy, budget-friendly meals that are sure to please. You barely need to plan your meal—just open the pantry and begin!

How to Read a Recipe

Before you start creating, it's important to read the recipe from beginning to end. This will help you avoid a cooking catastrophe!

Safe Kitchen Basics

Safety in the kitchen is the very first step. Make sure you begin with clean hands, tools, and surfaces. Any time you handle raw meat, wash your hands and any tools or surfaces the meat touched. Some of the recipes involve hot surfaces or sharp equipment. Have an adult nearby to help supervise and assist to keep you safe.

Never use hot or sharp things without an adult's permission.

Recipe Reading Checklist

- Do you have all the ingredients and tools?
- Do you understand the techniques listed in the directions?
- Do you have enough time to make the recipe?
- Have you read through the ingredients list thoroughly, in case you have dietary or allergy restrictions?
- Using metric tools? Here are conversions to make your recipe measure up.

Standard	Metric
1/4 teaspoon	1.25 grams or milliliters
1/2 teaspoon	2.5 g or mL
1 teaspoon	5 g or mL
1 tablespoon	15 g or mL
1/4 cup	57 g (dry) or 60 mL (liquid)
1/3 cup	75 g (dry) or 80 mL (liquid)
1/2 cup	114 g (dry) or 125 mL (liquid)
2/3 cup	150 g (dry) or 160 mL (liquid)
3/4 cup	170 g (dry) or 175 mL (liquid)
1 cup	227 g (dry) or 240 mL (liquid)
1 quart	950 mL

- All temperatures in this book are Fahrenheit. Use the chart here if you're cooking in Celsius.

Fahrenheit	Celsius
325°	160°
350°	180°
375°	190°
400°	200°
425°	220°
450°	230°

Breakfast Grilled Cheese

Grilled cheese—for breakfast?! Take your sandwich skills to the next level by making delicious, fluffy eggs. Then use them to fill an oozy, gooey cheese sandwich.

Prep time: 5 minutes • Cook time: 15 minutes • Makes 2 sandwiches

Ingredients

For the Scrambled Eggs:

2 large eggs

2 tablespoons milk

pinch of salt

2 teaspoons butter

For the Sandwiches:

4 slices American cheese

4 slices bread

2 tablespoons butter, room temperature

Tools

whisk

measuring cups/spoons

small mixing bowl

medium nonstick skillets

spatula

butter knife

Tip

Not an egg fan? You can make a grilled sandwich with a sweet and toasty flavor. Start at step 5. Spread nut butter onto the unbuttered side of a slice of bread. Top with jam or jelly, and then another slice of bread. Then skip to step 7 to finish. Add sliced banana or marshmallows for extra sweet flavor.

1. Whisk the eggs, milk, and salt together.
2. Ask an adult to place butter in the skillet and heat over medium. When the butter is melted, add the eggs.
3. Cook until the edges of the eggs begin to set. Then use the spatula to push the edges toward the center of the skillet.

4. Keep moving the eggs in the pan until there is no raw egg left. Once the eggs are cooked, set them aside.

5. Place the 4 slices of bread on a clean surface. Spread butter onto each slice. Then flip the slices butter-side-down.
6. Place a slice of cheese onto 2 slices of bread. Divide the eggs between them. Then top each with the remaining slices of bread, butter-side-up.
7. Ask an adult to heat a clean skillet over medium-low heat. Place the sandwiches on the hot pan. Cook until the bread begins to get golden brown and toasty, about 3 minutes. Then flip over with a spatula and cook another 3 minutes.
8. Remove from the pan, slice each sandwich in half, and serve immediately.

Variation You can easily replace the eggs, cheese, and butter in this recipe. Use vegan eggs, your favorite vegan cheese, and buttery spread to make the same fluffy and cheesy sandwich.

Cinnamon Roll Waffles

Cinnamon rolls are a delicious treat found mostly in North America and Northern Europe. They are made in many ways and have different names, such as cinnamon bun or cinnamon swirl. But here is a new way to eat them: as a waffle!

Prep time: 10 minutes • Cook time: 10 minutes • Makes 2 waffles

Ingredients

For the Waffles:

1 cup flour
1 ½ teaspoon baking powder
½ teaspoon salt
1 tablespoon brown sugar
1 tablespoon granulated sugar
2 teaspoons ground cinnamon
¾ cup milk
2 eggs
1 teaspoon vanilla
cooking spray

For the Maple Glaze:

1 tablespoon pure maple syrup
2 tablespoons melted butter
½ cup powdered sugar
2 tablespoons milk

Tools

whisk
measuring cups/spoons
large bowl
waffle iron
ladle
plate
small bowl
fork

1. Whisk the flour, baking powder, salt, brown sugar, granulated sugar, and cinnamon together in a bowl.
2. Add the milk, eggs, and vanilla. Stir until all the flour has absorbed the liquid. A few lumps are okay.
3. Have an adult preheat the waffle iron on medium-high. Spray the waffle iron with cooking spray.
4. Scoop about 2/3 cup of batter onto the waffle iron. Follow the waffle iron instructions to cook the waffle until it is golden brown and crispy. Continue cooking waffles until all the batter is used up.
5. To make the glaze, stir the maple syrup, melted butter, powdered sugar, and milk until smooth. Drizzle the glaze over the waffles before serving.

Variation Make this vegan by replacing the milk and butter with your favorite non-dairy milk and buttery spread. Substitute the 2 eggs by combining 2 tablespoons ground flax with ¼ cup water.

Variation No waffle iron? No problem! Make pancakes instead. Add 1 tablespoon of vegetable oil to your batter. Cook pancakes on a nonstick skillet heated to medium. Spritz the skillet with cooking spray and pour in ½ cup of batter. Let cook for 3 minutes or until bubbles begin to appear around the edges. Use a spatula to flip the pancake. Then cook another 2 to 3 minutes. Repeat until batter is gone.

Ramen Stir Fry

Instant ramen is a fast and easy lunch. But with an extra 10 minutes, you can dress it up and add loads more flavor. The key to the perfect stir fry is to prepare your sauce, noodles, and fillings before cooking. Pick your flavors, then get frying!

Prep time: 10 minutes • Cook time: 10 minutes • Makes 4 servings

Ingredients

6 ounces (170 grams) instant ramen noodles (flavor packets discarded)

6 cups very hot water

For the Sauce:

½ cup chicken or vegetable broth

⅓ cup stir fry sauce

For the Stir Fry:

2 tablespoon vegetable oil

3 cloves garlic, chopped

1 tablespoon fresh minced ginger

1 cup broccoli florets, fresh or frozen

¼ cup shredded carrots

1 can baby corn

1 can water chestnuts

Tools

large bowl

measuring cups/spoons

small bowl

whisk

colander

cutting board

chef's knife

large nonstick skillet

stirring spoon

1. Prep your noodles by placing them in a large bowl. Ask an adult to pour the hot water into the bowl. Set aside.
2. Whisk the broth and stir fry sauce together. Set aside.
3. Ask the adult to drain the noodles. Return them to the bowl and set aside.
4. Ask the adult to preheat the skillet on medium-high. Add the oil. Make sure all your ingredients are prepped and ready.
5. When the oil shimmers, add garlic and ginger. Stir carefully for 1 minute.
6. Add the broccoli. Cook for 1 to 2 minutes, until it turns bright green. Pour in the sauce, carrots, baby corn, and water chestnuts. Toss to coat the vegetables. Continue cooking for 1 minute.
7. Add the noodles. Stir for another 1 to 2 minutes or until the sauce thickens and the ingredients are coated well. Remove from heat and serve immediately.

Variation Add cooked chicken for some protein. If you're meat-free, add tofu, seitan, or chickpeas.

Baked Ranch Chicken Bites

Ranch is one of the most popular condiments out there. Combine it with one of the most popular kid-friendly favorites—chicken nuggets! These chicken bites are made with panko bread crumbs, a special Japanese breadcrumb that you can find in your grocery store. They are lighter than regular bread crumbs and have a fantastic crunch when you make and bake these chicken bites!

Prep time: 10 minutes • Cook time: 25 minutes • Makes 4 servings

Ingredients

2 tablespoons grated Parmesan cheese

1 cup panko bread crumbs

1-ounce (28-gram) package ranch dressing mix

1 egg

1 pound (454 grams) chicken breast tenders

dipping sauces, such as ranch, barbecue, ketchup, or sriracha

Tools

parchment paper-lined baking sheet

two shallow dishes, such as pie plates or round cake pans

fork

paper towels

1. Ask an adult to preheat oven to 350 degrees.
2. In a shallow dish, combine the Parmesan cheese, panko bread crumbs, and ranch dressing mix. Use a fork to stir. Set aside.
3. Crack an egg into the second shallow dish. Use the fork to scramble the egg.
4. Pat the chicken dry with paper towels. Dip a piece of chicken in the egg, coating it on all sides. Let the extra egg drip off the chicken and back into the dish. Then set the chicken into the bread crumb mixture. Coat the chicken thoroughly.
5. Set chicken on the baking sheet. Repeat step 4 with the remaining pieces of chicken. Keep chicken pieces at least 1 inch apart. Wash hands thoroughly after handling chicken.
6. Bake for about 25 minutes or until the chicken is fully cooked and no longer pink inside. Serve the chicken bites hot with your favorite dipping sauce.

Variation You don't need chicken to make these crispy bites! Instead of chicken, use extra-firm tofu that has been drained and pressed. Cut the tofu into 2-inch (5-centimeter) cubes. Toss with 1 ½ tablespoons of olive oil in a large bowl. In another large bowl, combine ½ cup panko bread crumbs, ½ teaspoon kosher salt, ¼ teaspoon ground black pepper, 2 tablespoons of nutritional yeast, and 1 teaspoon each onion powder, garlic powder, dried dill, and dried parsley. Toss the tofu in the bread crumb mixture. Bake at 425 degrees for about 25 minutes.

Very Veggie Soup

Bragging that you ate all your vegetables won't be hard with this veggie-packed soup! This recipe uses a mix of fresh, frozen, and canned veggies. Swap out those you don't like for those you love. Sub in any you have on hand for those not already available. Maybe you'll find a new favorite!

Prep time: 10 minutes • Cook time: 30 minutes • Makes 8 servings

Ingredients

1 tablespoon olive oil
1 medium onion, diced
1 cup carrots, diced
2 cloves garlic, minced
1 teaspoon salt
½ teaspoon ground black pepper
1 tablespoon dried Italian seasoning
6 ounces (0.2 liters) tomato paste
64 ounces (2 L) vegetable broth
2 medium russet potatoes, diced
15 ounces (0.4 L) canned crushed tomatoes
15 ounces canned diced tomatoes, undrained
1 cup frozen green beans
1 cup frozen sweet corn kernels

Tools

measuring cups/spoons
large pot
stirring spoon
can opener
colander

1. Measure the olive oil into a large pot. Then ask an adult to set the pot on the stove and heat to medium-high.
2. Place the onions and carrots in the pot. Stir occasionally until the onions begin to soften, around 8 to 10 minutes.
3. Add the garlic. Stir and cook for another minute.
4. Flavor with the salt, pepper, and Italian seasoning. Stir in the tomato paste. Then pour in the vegetable broth.
5. Add the diced potatoes and both cans of tomatoes. Bring to a boil. Then reduce heat to medium-low so the soup simmers gently. Cook for 20 to 25 minutes, or until the potatoes are tender.
6. Add the green beans and corn and cook an additional 5 minutes.

Variation Add different veggies to the mix! Zucchini, celery, mushrooms, summer squash, leeks, and fresh green beans can go in the pot with the carrots and onions. Trade the canned and frozen options for fresh. Try out other root vegetables besides potatoes—sweet potatoes, winter squash, and turnips are good options. Leafy greens, such as kale, spinach, or Swiss chard, can be added with the frozen veggies.

Tip

Any cook worth their salt knows how to season what they make. Salt can make or break a recipe. Not enough salt and you'll be missing the flavor; too much salt and you'll be gulping down glasses of water. It's very important to taste your food before you serve it. If you add salt, start with a little at a time. It's easy to add more salt. Too-salty food is hard to fix.

Broccoli Cheese Hand Pies

Pasties were first made as a lunch for workers in Cornwall, England. In the United States, they're called hand pies. More like a pot pie without the pot, these handheld pockets are perfect for holding your favorite flavors.

Prep time: 10 minutes • Cook time: 25 minutes • Makes 4 hand pies

Ingredients

1 package frozen puff pastry dough sheets, defrosted

1 cup shredded cheddar cheese

1 cup steamed broccoli florets

1 egg

Tools

cutting board

pizza cutter

measuring cups/spoons

parchment paper-lined baking sheet

whisk

small bowl

pastry brush

knife

1. Ask an adult to preheat oven to 375 degrees.
2. Roll out the puff pastry onto the cutting board. Shape it into a horizontal rectangle.
3. Ask an adult to cut the rectangle in half vertically using a pizza cutter. Then have them cut the 2 pieces in half again to make 4 rectangles.
4. Put 1 tablespoon of cheddar cheese on the top half of each rectangle. Leave a ½-inch (1.3-cm) rim around the edges.
5. Divide the broccoli and remaining cheese between each rectangle.

6. Close and seal the pastries for baking. Fold the bottom half of the pastry up and over the top of the fillings. Press the edges down firmly to seal.

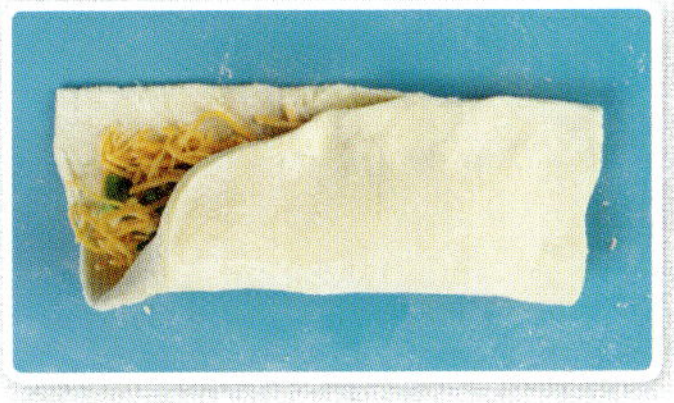

7. Set each pastry onto the parchment paper-lined baking sheet. Make sure there is at least an inch between each.
8. Whisk the egg in a small bowl. Use a pastry brush to paint the tops of the hand pies with egg.
9. Ask an adult to make 3 small slits on top of the pies with a knife. This will allow steam to escape while they bake.
10. Bake for 20–25 minutes or until the tops are golden brown. Let cool for 5 minutes before serving.

Sloppy Joe Totchos

You've heard of sloppy joes. You've heard of nachos. But totchos?! Puffy potatoes are baked to crispy perfection. Then they are topped with the filling of your favorite messy sandwich. Finish them with melted cheese and pickles to make this a perfect dinner.

Prep time: 10 minutes • Cook time: 40 minutes • Makes 6-8 servings

Ingredients

1 tablespoon olive oil

1 bell pepper, chopped

½ large onion, chopped

32-ounce (910-gram) package frozen tater tots

1 pound ground beef

1 package sloppy joe seasoning

8 ounces (0.2 L) canned tomato sauce

½ cup barbecue sauce

⅓ cup water

1 tsp salt

1 cup shredded cheddar cheese

½ cup bread and butter pickles

Tools

large baking sheet lined with parchment paper

large skillet

measuring cups/spoons

spatula

1. Ask an adult to preheat oven to 450 degrees Fahrenheit.

2. With the adult's help, heat the oil in a large skillet over medium heat. Add the pepper and onion. Cook for 5 to 7 minutes, stirring occasionally until the vegetables begin to soften.

3. Meanwhile, place tater tots on the baking sheet and put in the oven. Set a timer for 25 minutes.

3. Add ground beef to the skillet. Use a spatula to break apart the beef. Cook until no longer pink, about 5 to 7 minutes. Ask the adult to carefully drain any excess fat in the pan.

4. Sprinkle the sloppy joe seasoning into the pan. Stir well. Then add the tomato sauce, barbecue sauce, and water. Simmer for 10 to 15 minutes, until the sauce thickens.

5. When the tater tots are golden brown, ask the adult to remove them from the oven. Sprinkle the hot tots with salt.

6. Spoon the sloppy joe mixture evenly over the tater tots. Layer cheese over the top. Ask the adult to put the tots back in the oven to melt the cheese.

7. Remove from the oven. Top with pickles. Eat!

Variation Veggie lovers can still get sloppy with these totchos! Replace the meat with 2 cups of cooked lentils or black beans.

Tomato-Basil Pasta

Pasta and tomato sauce are a classic combo. Sweet tomatoes and fresh basil make a sauce that comes together easily and quickly.

Prep time: 10 minutes • Cook time: 20 minutes • Makes 6-8 servings

Ingredients

2 tablespoons kosher salt
16 ounces (450 grams) dry fusilli pasta
3 tablespoons olive oil
1 onion, diced
2 cloves garlic, minced
2 pints cherry or grape tomatoes
¼ teaspoon sugar
10 leaves fresh basil
½ cup grated Parmesan cheese, plus more for serving

Tools

large pot
measuring cups/spoons
long stirring spoon
large skillet
colander

1. Fill a large pot with water and add the salt. Ask an adult to bring the water to a boil on high heat.
2. Add the pasta to the pot of water. Stir gently to keep the noodles from sticking together. Cook for 10 minutes, or until the noodles are tender. Ask an adult to help you test the noodles—they're hot!
3. While the pasta cooks, you can get your sauce started. Pour the olive oil into the skillet and have the adult heat the skillet over medium heat. Add the onion and stir.
4. Cook the onion for 5 minutes until it starts to soften. Add the garlic and stir for another minute.
5. Add the tomatoes and sugar. Cook and stir for about 10 minutes. The tomatoes will burst, and the juice will make a sauce.
6. Ask the adult to drain the cooked pasta. Dump the pasta into the tomato sauce and cook for 2 minutes, coating the pasta well.
7. Turn off the burner. Stir in half of the Parmesan cheese. When it's melted, repeat with the rest of the cheese.
8. Stack the basil leaves on top of each other. Roll the leaves into a tube. Then carefully cut the basil into ribbons.

9. Toss the basil with the pasta. Then divide the pasta into bowls and sprinkle with cheese.

Variation If you don't have fresh tomatoes or basil on hand, no worries. You can use a can of undrained diced tomatoes and 1 teaspoon of dried basil instead.

Tip

Do you really need 2 tablespoons of salt? Yes! It's important to add salt when you cook pasta. Dried pasta by itself is pretty boring—usually it's just water and flour. The pasta will absorb only some of the salt in the cooking water.

Tripleberry Smoothie

Thick, creamy, and refreshing—you can enjoy this filling smoothie as a snack or even a breakfast! A handful of berries and a quick blend are all you need to start slurping.

Prep time: 5 minutes • Cook time: 0 minutes • Makes 2 smoothies

Ingredients

1 cup milk

2/3 cup vanilla yogurt

1 banana, peeled

½ cup frozen strawberries

½ cup frozen blueberries

½ cup frozen raspberries

handful frozen berries, for garnish

Tools

measuring cups

blender

glasses, for serving

1. Measure and pour all the ingredients into a blender.
2. Ask an adult to blend on high until smooth. If the smoothie seems too thick, add a little more milk and blend again.
3. Pour into 2 glasses and top with extra berries.

Variations

- Make it a PB and J smoothie by adding 2 tablespoons of peanut butter.
- Feeling tropical? Use pineapple juice in place of the milk.
- Add 1 cup of raw spinach before you blend for a healthier smoothie. You won't taste it—promise!
- If you eat vegan, be sure to use a non-dairy milk and yogurt.

Banana Bites

Looking for a fast and tasty recipe to satisfy your snack attack? This recipe is roll-and-go! Customize it to fit your favorite flavors and textures.

Prep time: 5 minutes • Cook time: 0 minutes • Makes 6 bites

Ingredients

8-inch (20-cm) tortilla

¼ cup nut or sunflower seed butter

2 tablespoons mix-ins of your choice

banana

Tools

cutting board

measuring cup/spoons

spatula

knife

1. Set the tortilla flat on a clean cutting board.
2. Spread the nut butter onto the tortilla. Leave a small rim around the edges.
3. Drizzle or sprinkle the mix-ins evenly over the nut butter.
4. Peel the banana and place in the center. Roll the tortilla around the banana.
5. Slice into 6 pieces and serve.

Variation What can you add to your Banana Bites? Get creative! Here are some ideas:

jam

mini chocolate chips

mini marshmallows

chopped nuts

granola or trail mix

honey

crumbled graham crackers

coconut flakes

sliced strawberries

Ice-Cream S'morewiches

You don't need a campfire to snack on the best outdoor treat! Summer's best dessert can be enjoyed year-round. Have fun making your own s'more ice-cream sandwiches indoors.

Prep time: 15 minutes • Cook time: 0 minutes • Makes 6 sandwiches

Ingredients

1.5-quart (1.4-liter) container vanilla ice cream

12 graham cracker squares

1 cup mini chocolate chips

1 cup marshmallow fluff

toppings, such as sprinkles, cereal, crushed waffle cones, pulverized freeze dried fruit, or chocolate curls

Tools

freezer-safe dish or pan

spoon

small bowls

1. Let the ice cream sit out at room temperature for 15 minutes, to soften.
2. Place the dish or pan in a flat part of your freezer.
3. Scoop and spread ¼ to ½ cup of ice cream onto a graham cracker square.
4. Sprinkle about 1 tablespoon of chocolate chips over the ice cream. Place the graham cracker and ice cream on the dish in the freezer. Repeat until the pan is full or until you have as many s'morewiches as you want. Freeze for 30 minutes.
5. Remove pan from freezer. Spread 2 tablespoons of marshmallow fluff over the chocolate chips on each graham cracker.
6. Top each s'morewich with another graham cracker. Return to freezer for another 30 minutes.
7. Pour toppings onto a shallow plate. Dip the exposed edges of the ice cream into the toppings of your choice.

Tip

Spray the spoon with a little cooking spray or butter to make the marshmallow fluff less sticky and more spreadable.

Fruity Ice Pops

Perfect for a hot summer day, and healthy too, these popsicles are both colorful and delicious. The frozen treats in the freezer section of your grocery store are full of artificial flavors and added sugar. By making your own, you know exactly what you're eating.

Prep time: 10 minutes • Cook time: 0 hours • Makes 6 ice pops

Ingredients

6 strawberries
½ cup blueberries
1 cup orange-pineapple juice

Tools

knife
cutting board
ice-pop mold
measuring cups
ice-pop sticks

1. Ask an adult to cut the stems off the strawberries. Then slice them into ½-inch- (1.3-cm)-thick slices.
2. Fill the ice-pop molds with strawberries and blueberries. Leave about ½ inch of space at the top of the molds.
3. Add the juice to each mold. Pour juice to just the tops of the berries.
4. Place ice-pop sticks in the molds. Then place in freezer for at least 4 hours, or until firm. Release the ice pops by running warm water over the mold.

Tip

Want to make your very own freezies? Have an adult blend all the ingredients. Then carefully pour into ice-pop pouches before putting in the freezer.

But you don't need to have an ice-pop mold or special pouches to make these! Use an ice-cube tray or even small paper cups. Let the ice pops set slightly before adding the sticks.

Cooking Glossary

colander (KAH-luhn-duhr)—a kitchen tool with gaps or holes for washing or draining food

dice (DIES)—to cut into small cubes

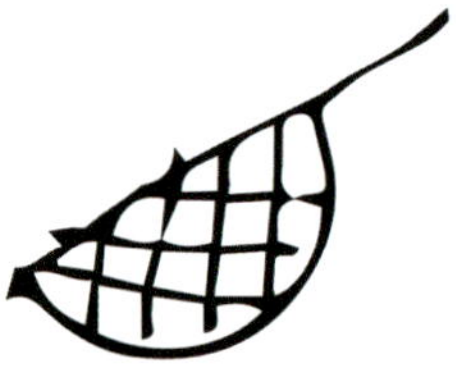

drizzle (DRIZ-uhl)—to pour in light, steady drops

floret (flo-RET)—small pieces of vegetables, such as broccoli or cauliflower, separated from a larger head

ladle (LAY-duhl)—a deep-bowled spoon with a long handle used to serve or transport liquids

mince (MINS)—to cut into very small pieces

mold (MOLD)—a cavity used to shape food

parchment paper (PARCH-muhnt PAY-puhr)—paper sold in rolls used for baking

preheat (pre-HEET)—to heat an oven to a designated temperature before baking

prep (PREP)—to prepare ingredients before cooking or baking

seal (SEEL)—to close something up

set (SET)—hardened or solidified

whisk (WISK)—a wire kitchen tool used for mixing food

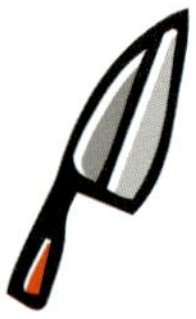

Tools

8-inch (20.3-centimeter) square baking pan

blender

can opener

colander

cutting board

knife

large baking sheet

large pot

measuring cups/spoons

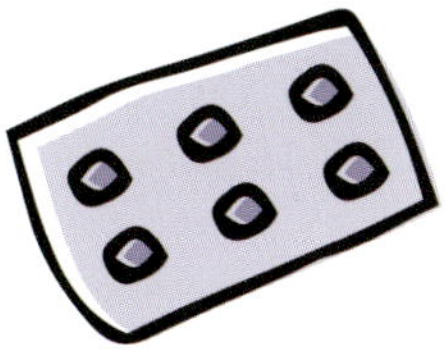

ladle

mixing bowls

mixing spoons

nonstick pots and pans

popsicle mold

scraping spatula

turning spatula

waffle iron

whisk

Read More

Blake, Arena. *Awesome Edible Kids Crafts: 75 Super-Fun All-Natural Projects for Kids to Make and Eat.* Salem, MA: Page Street Publishing Co., 2019.

Lamielle, Pierra A. *The Munchy Munchy Cookbook for Kids.* Sanger, CA: Familius, 2019.

Spears, Anthony. *Chef Junior: A Real Food Guide to Learning How to Cook—By Kids For Kids.* New York: Sterling Publishing Co., Inc., 2020.

Internet Sites

Academy of Nutrition and Dietetics: Teaching Kids to Cook
https://www.eatright.org/homefoodsafety/four-steps/cook/teaching-kids-to-cook

Cooking Party Games
https://www.thespruce.com/kids-chef-and-cooking-party-games-2104586

Recipes Kids Can Make
https://www.foodnetwork.com/recipes/packages/recipes-for-kids/cooking-with-kids/recipes-kids-can-make